Connect to the YOU Within

—

SHELLY WILSON

Connect to the YOU Within
By Shelly Wilson
Copyright © 2013 Shelly R. Wilson
www.shellyrwilson.com
Bluebird House Publications

Cover design and formatting
by Lloyd Matthew Thompson
www.StarfieldPress.com

Shelly R. Wilson
Intuitive Medium ~ Reiki Master ~ Spiritual Teacher
36511 S 4450 Rd
Vinita, OK 74301
(918) 782-4778
www.shellyrwilson.com
shelly@shellyrwilson.com

Connect to the YOU Within

uplifting in such a way that I was compelled to really hear on a deeper level what she told me during the reading, and her insight was spot on to the point that no longer could my stubborn brain deny it. I knew...she knew. We knew. Now, I needed to *own* what I knew!

This book offers ample opportunities to reconnect with the "You" you may have once been, or want to be, or maybe never had the opportunity to become in the first place. With loving insight and gentle, yet firm, guidance, Shelly fills each chapter with personal experiences, practical wisdom and even meditations, journaling exercises, affirmations and "uplifts" that are sure to have you feeling more empowered and more connected to that inner light you may have been ignoring. Shelly helps you free that light and let it shine.

I am a smart girl. I often know what I need to change and what steps I need to take to make my life better. Yet knowledge is useless without action, and I find myself dimming my own light or avoiding my own gifts, as if in fear that my greatness might swallow me whole, even as I ache to step into that fullness of who I really am. Fear of failure, fear of success, fear of change...though we all may understand these forms of resistance, we don't have the proper skills and emotional support to knock them down or leap over them.

When it comes to connecting to that unique and amazing "You" within, we sometimes need the help of

~ Foreword ~

Who am I? Funny how we rarely ask that question when we are children, as if we know then, during our most formative years, that we are exactly who we are and who we want to be. Yet as we grow older, we not only lose our sense of self, we lose our direction and sense of purpose and destiny as our consciousness becomes overwhelmed with the day-to-day grind of making a living.

But is that... a life?

If you have been feeling trapped in the confines of your own limitations, Shelly Wilson can help you not only find your way back to yourself, but back to the path you came here in this incarnation to walk, and to walk with joy and purpose and happiness. I have known Shelly for a while, and she recently did a reading for me that truly served to realign me with what my inner guide already had been telling me, but my intellect and reasoning mind refused to acknowledge. Shelly's energy is infectious and

*This book is dedicated to all who are embarking
or continuing on their own spiritual journey.*

I am grateful for my family and friends and ALL of the
experiences I have had.
I acknowledge your presence in my life,
I value our relationship,
I appreciate your support and
I love you tremendously.

I am so thankful for YOU!

~ CONTENTS ~

FOREWORD ~...9

INTRODUCTION ~...25

CHAPTER 1 ~ YOU ARE NOT ALONE 35

CHAPTER 2 ~ OPENING YOUR HEART TO LOVE...........47

CHAPTER 3 ~ THE TRUTH OF WHO YOU ARE.........................57

CHAPTER 4 ~ BEING MINDFULLY PRESENT 69

CHAPTER 5 ~ CONSCIOUSLY CREATING 83

CHAPTER 6 ~ MAKING CONSCIOUS CONNECTIONS 97

CHAPTER 7 ~ AWAKENING TO YOUR PURPOSE 111

CHAPTER 8 ~ SHINING YOUR LIGHT BRIGHT 125

CONCLUSION ~...135

ABOUT SHELLY ~..139

guides both human and non-human to kick our butts into gear to move past the resistance and the fear and the doubt. Shelly Wilson's *Connect to the You Within* is really— if you think about it— a life-saver. Oh, it won't teach you how to save yourself if you are choking on a peach pit (Google "give yourself the Heimlich" for that), but it will save you from living a half-life that is small and dim and mediocre when you could be living the fullest, most powerful and positive expression of who you are, and who you were meant to be.

Read this wonderful guide for the spirit and the mind, and then ask yourself "Who am I?" and be ready to fully step into yourself to shine that light that only YOU can shine.

Marie D. Jones
Author/Producer/Screenwriter/Speaker/Researcher

www.MarieDJones.com

Bestselling author of *Destiny Vs. Choice: The Scientific and Spiritual Evidence Behind Fate and Free Will*

Additional books Marie has authored:

2013: End of Days or a New Beginning - Envisioning the World After the Events of 2012

PSIence: How New Discoveries in Quantum Physics and New Science May Explain the Existence of Paranormal Phenomenon

Supervolcano: The Catastrophic Event That Changed the Course of Human History

This Book Is From the Future: A Journey Through Portals, Relativity, Wormholes and Other Adventures in Time Travel

The Trinity Secret: The Power of Three and the Code of Creation

The Déjà vu Enigma: A Journey Through the Anomalies of Mind, Memory and Time

11:11 - The Time Prompt Phenomenon: The Meaning Behind Mysterious Signs, Sequences and Synchronicities

The Resonance Key: Exploring the Links Between Vibration, Consciousness and the Zero Point Grid

This is not a book you'll read leisurely and ponder taking action steps to change your life at some distant point in the future. This powerful book will immediately catapult you into meditations, journaling, affirmations and new insights that reconnect you to your higher self, your soul's mission, and your purpose here on earth. The exercises, questions, suggestions and uplifting messages within these pages will inspire you to move through your pain and fear and embrace your greatest potential in every area of life. Kudos to Shelly Wilson for making spirituality so accessible, practical and easy to master.

Sue Frederick
Intuitive and Bestselling author of *I See Your Dream Job; I See Your Soul Mate* and *Bridges to Heaven: True Stories of Loved Ones on the Other Side (St. Martin's Press)*

www.SueFrederick.com

Nothing can begin without first beginning with your*self*. From the action of getting up to walk across the room for a glass of water, to making a definite change in this world— it all begins with YOU.

YOU are the one who sparks the thought that fires your muscles into action, YOU are the one who launches the thought-energy of manifestation into the Universe, YOU are the one who initializes the effort to create the wave that will ripple out and change your household, your neighborhood, your city, your state, your country, your planet.

If you want anything outside yourself to be different, look first *inside* yourself. I feel this cannot be stressed enough— repeated over and over, until it grows into our natural, knee-jerk response. In *Connect to the YOU Within*, Shelly does a magnificent job of guiding us toward this habit in a smooth and logical manner that is as gentle as it is humbling.

I've had the honor of knowing and working with Shelly personally for years now, and have never ceased to be amazed and inspired in my own journey by the energy and enthusiasm she demonstrates in all areas of her path, regardless how small or how large. Her Heart is a powerhouse that shows no signs of stopping for decades to come— and intends to shine Light on as many souls as possible before all is said and done.

So you're holding the book. Are you ready to open yourself to *yourself?* I'm not going to sugarcoat— it can be scary at times, it can be emotional at times, but each round you go with yourself, you come out *that* much more empowered. That much more *YOU.*

How wonderful does *that* sound to YOU?

Lloyd Matthew Thompson
Author of *The Galaxy Healer's Guide* and
The Energy Anthology chakra series.

www.GalaxyEnergy.org
www.StarfieldPress.com

The task of loving ourselves is perhaps the most urgent and glorious work we can undertake. For many, it is the task they took birth for; for others, it is an essential component of fulfilling their roles as parents and children, friends and lovers, neighbors and members of our global village. But this task can be made difficult by a culture where productivity, superficiality, and prejudice threaten and where the life of our feelings and sense of purpose is often undervalued. In addition, as a therapist, I know that along the path to loving ourselves we meet the dragons of shame and inner-criticism that inhabit our inner worlds distorting how we view our bodies, feelings, relationships, and work in the world.

In short, we need help; we need elders; we need lovers. We need to create a space for ourselves nurtured by a different voice. Sweet, profoundly respectful of the autonomy and spirit of her readers—Shelly Wilson has provided that voice and nurturance.

In a world of outer authorities aplenty, Shelly Wilson invites us to open the door to our own hearts, our own wisdom— our teacher-within. However, she doesn't just drop us off at the train station; she sits alongside us guiding us ever inward through meditation, affirmation, journaling, inspiration, and most of all, her loving presence.

David Bedrick, J.D., Dipl. PW

Author of *Talking Back to Dr. Phil: Alternatives to Mainstream Psychology*

www.DavidBedrick.com

Connect to the YOU Within

—

SHELLY WILSON

I wish to ask you…

Are you listening and paying attention to the guidance you are receiving?

Do you acknowledge this knowingness fully and completely?

.

We do not believe in ourselves
until someone reveals that deep inside us
something is valuable,
worth listening to, worthy of our trust,
sacred to our touch.
Once we believe in ourselves we can risk curiosity,
wonder, spontaneous delight,
or any experience that reveals the human spirit.

~ e.e. cummings

~ Introduction ~

As an Intuitive Medium, Reiki Master and Spiritual Teacher, my personal mission is to assist others on their own journey into consciousness while encouraging them to live an authentic life through awareness and empowerment. Coming from a place of respect, truth, integrity and love, I honor your free will and recognize that you are co-creating your reality with the Universe. My intention is to bring understanding, help you to heal from the past and realize your full potential. I invite you to begin your life in a new way and tap into your inner power as you explore who you really are. Refrain from simply existing and elect to live your life fully without regret. It is time to let go of the past, live in the present and look to the future for it is this attitude that will transform you.

What you need to know about the past
is that no matter what has happened,
it has all worked together to bring you to this very moment.
And this is the moment
you can choose to make everything new.
Right now.
~ **Author Unknown**

I have chosen to write this book to assist you in recognizing that your soul is already awake. Your mind and physical body simply need to connect with the knowingness of your soul— the YOU within. The topics covered in this book were originally visited in my DailyOM course, Opening Your Heart to Love. Having written the course a year ago, my guides recently nudged me to revisit what I had written and to revise and update the material. I realized that a course has the energy of studying and coursework, which may leave many people with the feeling of obligation or commitment so they choose not to participate. The energy of a book in my perception is completely different; it is simply meant to be read and absorbed without doing any "work" per se.

There are a couple of ideas that I would like to suggest to increase your chances of having the outcome you desire. The first and foremost is to be kind to yourself. Allow yourself the opportunity to take baby steps. As you shift your perception, you will change your experiences, including those in the past, the ones you are presently experiencing and those that have yet to happen. This involves altering your mindset and attitude as well as your thoughts, words and actions. I recommend identifying an accountability partner or two. This friend or family member should be someone who is willing to listen to you and also tell you the truth when you ask for advice (and even when you don't directly ask). They should be someone that you trust and can count on to be there for you. They are your support and will help motivate you.

Meditate

In addition, I believe that meditation is important. Take time each day to connect with YOU— your inner self— through meditation. Whether you enjoy sitting silently in reflection, listening to a guided meditation, spending time outdoors in nature or going for a walking awareness meditation; meditation will enhance your life tremendously. For some individuals, reading is a form of meditation. The intent of meditation is to just BE and listen. Allowing yourself to listen to the guidance you are receiving and to be present in the moment will assist you tremendously.

Perhaps, you may even be guided, just as I am, to pause from what you are doing, close your eyes, sit silently for a few minutes to connect, and then resume the activity. Throughout the day and even now as I am writing, I will do exactly that. I stop when I am guided to. Although it may be just for a few minutes, those minutes have an extremely powerful effect. Not only do I feel refreshed and energized, but my concentration is typically enhanced, and I am able to accomplish more in less time.

Journal

Journaling daily is recommended as it will assist you in recognizing who you were, who you are and who you are becoming. Write down your thoughts, feelings and emotions as you are guided to do so throughout the day. Pay attention to bodily sensations as well. Read back through what you have written whenever you are guided to.

Keep in mind that there is no right way or wrong way to journal— only your way. You may opt to keep a handwritten notebook or maintain a document on your computer or even both as I do. Do not constrain your expression by feeling obligated to write for a specific amount of time. Simply allow the words to flow. For many individuals, their blog is their journal. I can attest that journaling assisted me greatly with my awakening and opening up to Spirit. Plus, it really helps me to remember my dreams.

Daily Message to Uplift

For each day, I am offering a message to uplift your Spirit using Doreen Virtue's Healing with the Angels oracle cards as a Divination tool to assist me in the process. The cards I pulled for each day are displayed in bold. The accompanying message is my insightful interpretation. I encourage you to go within to interpret the meaning of the messages for you specifically.

Since we each have freewill, practicing discernment and acknowledging what feels right to you is essential. If any of the information I have provided does not resonate with you, please practice discernment and choose not to accept it for yourself. In other words, accept what resonates and discard the rest. Do not feel like it has to be all or nothing.

I invite you to awaken

to the truth

of who you are

as you connect

to the YOU within.

Focusing on the act of breathing
clears the mind of all daily distractions
and clears our energy enabling us to better connect
with the Spirit within.

~ Author Unknown

~ Chapter 1 ~
You Are Not Alone

As long as I can remember, I have always felt different. I was conditioned as a child to mind my manners, keep my opinions to myself, and do as I was told. I lacked confidence and self-esteem.

A significant memory I have of myself is when I was about 6 years old. I was playing on the playground near a swing set at elementary school by myself. I was being taunted by some of the other children because I had silver caps on all of my teeth. I can see the dress I am wearing and the way my blond hair flipped up on the ends. I seldom smiled and would keep my head tucked down. This image continues to surface in my consciousness. I acknowledge that this little girl will always remain with me as she is a part of who I am.

I recognize that being the new kid at school on numerous occasions played a contributing role with my confidence issues. I was the quiet smart kid who liked to read. To fit in with others, I learned to listen and observe. I learned to think before speaking. Although I did have a few friends, I still felt alone most of the time.

Fast forward many years, I found my voice and realized that what I say does matter. I began acknowledging the guidance that I had been receiving all along. I now know that I was never truly alone. Reflecting on those years, perhaps I was special rather than different. As I began connecting to my soul, I awakened to the truth of who I am. Choosing to change my perception of the experiences I had, I inevitably shift the energy of those experiences.

I realize now that all of my challenges and triumphs were actually opportunities for learning and growth. I actually planned each and every one of them prior to this incarnation so that I could be the person that I am today. With that being said, I believe that all is as it should be in each and every moment.

The magnitude of life is overwhelming.
Angels are here to help us take it peace by peace.
~ **Levende Waters**

Every human being desires to not only feel loved, but to give love as well. It's innate within each of us to want to connect with others, to want to be open and to live an authentic life. We want to love and to be loved in return. Expressing love and sharing kindness takes such a small effort yet has an enormous effect. This ripple of love surpasses anything anyone could imagine if they would just simply allow this love to come in. I know that anything is possible with love— as love is all there really is. There is an essential need for people to grow together, support one another and walk together as both human companions and soul companions.

Why should I stay at the bottom of a well,
when a strong rope is in my hand?
~ Rumi

This quote by Rumi reminds me that we are not alone, and that there is a great amount of love and support available to each one of us. The rope is an analogy for our support system. Our family and friends are in our lives for a reason. Sometimes, they do not know that we need assistance so it is crucial to actually ask for help when we need it. In turn, offer your support when you can to others. Our friends are the souls we have chosen to accompany us on our journey in this lifetime, and are an important part of our learning and growth.

Make yourself familiar with the angels,
and behold them frequently in spirit;
for, without being seen,
they are present with you.
~ **St Francis of Sales**

In addition to the support network of our friends and family, each one of us has a guardian angel, who has been with us since the moment we were born. We also have access to all of the Archangels and Ascended Masters. The angels continue to remind us that they are with us standing by— ready, willing, and able to assist. All we have to do is ask for their assistance as they cannot intervene in our freewill choices unless the consequences are dire, and it is not our time to depart the earthly plane. We can call upon them for assistance at any time as they are available to everyone. You do not need to reference any particular Archangel or Ascended Master to receive support. Simply say, *"Archangels/Ascended Masters, I call upon you now!"*

However, if you do wish to call upon a specific Archangel based on their specialties, I have provided a short list for you here. Please know that there are many others. I encourage you to seek resources to learn more about the Archangels and Ascended Masters.

- **Michael** ~ strength, courage, protection

- **Raphael** ~ healing

- **Gabriel** ~ communication

- **Uriel** ~ knowledge, understanding

- **Chamuel** ~ peace

- **Ariel** ~ manifesting

- **Metatron** ~ sacred geometry, esoteric healing

- **Azrael** ~ transitions, healing

- **Jophiel** ~ beautifying thoughts, clearing clutter

Therefore, as an example, you would say, *"Archangel Michael, I call upon you now. Please provide me with strength, courage, and protection during this time."*

Meditation is an excellent tool to connect with YOU. In doing so, you are connecting with your Higher Self, your angels, your guides and even your loved ones in the spiritual realm. Meditation comes in many forms. You may choose to listen to a guided meditation, simply sit quietly, or even go for a walk. Each of these methods ultimately has the same end result— connecting you to your soul. It is necessary for you to select the appropriate form of meditation that resonates with you.

Good for the body is the work of the body,
and good for the soul is the work of the soul,
and good for either is the work of the other.
~ **Henry David Thoreau**

Cultivating a relationship with your guides is beneficial and refreshing. While studying advanced mediumship with Lisa Williams, the course's exercises gave me the motivation I needed to strengthen and cultivate the relationship that I have with each one of my guides. I recognize that they are patiently waiting for me to communicate with them regularly rather than rely on them periodically. I previously viewed them as a collective rather than separate entities. Now, I feel the tremendous need to recognize their individuality.

I have opted to go into meditation on several occasions with the specific intent to learn more about each one of my guides. I chose to do so silently rather than using a guided meditation. They presented themselves to me one at a time, and I acknowledged their presence. I recognize that I definitely need to spend time daily cultivating the relationship that I have with each one of them. My guides assist me daily in my work. Not only do they encourage my writing, but they are also my support team and biggest fans. Their loving guidance continues to remind me that affecting one person will have a ripple effect with many. I feel like it is important to mention that it is extremely comfortable and minimal effort is required to connect with my guides. Doing so is as effortless as picking up the telephone to call a friend only no charges are incurred for making the connection.

I pay attention to the nudges and whispers and will pause to meditate as I am guided to. There is no minimum or maximum time limit required to do so. I simply allow myself to be. In doing so, I feel the Divine energy that surrounds me. I allow it to envelop my entire being, and I give thanks for All That Is. Being thankful for this moment and every moment, I allow the love to flow freely through me and around me and I simply breathe. My heart overflows with gratitude and joy. I am conscious of being present in this moment. I recognize the guidance I am receiving. I am allowing myself to simply breathe. I acknowledge and appreciate that I am not alone for my angels and guides are with me always.

"Connecting to YOU" Meditation

Take a moment to just BE. Sit in a chair with your back straight and your palms up (open to receiving). Close your eyes. Relax. Breathe in deeply and exhale.

Imagine yourself in the most beautiful tranquil place. This is your safe haven, your nirvana, your paradise. Your senses are heightened as you conceptualize this utopia.

You may be wandering in a lush green pasture of tall grass blowing gently in the wind. The smell of earth and nature fills your lungs. The blue sky is above you and there are rolling hills in the distance beckoning you. As you continue to wander, it is time to ground your energy.

Envision tree roots coming up through your feet and a vine wrapping around your legs. This vine is extending upwards into your root chakra, moving up into your sacral chakra, moving up and extending into your solar plexus chakra and resting in your heart chakra grounding you in Mother Earth. Now, envision white light from Source consciousness coming in through your crown chakra, down into your third eye chakra, down into your throat chakra, and meeting with Mother Earth energy at your heart chakra. You are grounded to Earth and to Light.

Be mindful of your breaths. Feel your chest expand with the inhalations. Feel your chest deflate with the exhalations. Feel the love you have within you. Allow the essence of you to unfold and surround you.

This beautiful Divine energy surrounds your being. Allow it to envelop you fully. Open your heart to love. Be thankful for this moment and every moment. Allow this gratitude and love to flow freely through you and around you as you simply breathe.

Affirm ~ *My heart overflows with gratitude and joy. I am conscious of being present in this moment. I recognize the guidance I will be receiving. I am allowing myself to simply breathe. I acknowledge and appreciate that I am not alone for my angels and guides are with me always.*

Now, pay attention to the guidance you are receiving. This guidance may be from your Higher Self, your angels, and your guides. There is no need to determine the source. Simply receive and listen.

Express your gratitude for receiving the guidance you have received. Once again, be mindful of your breaths. Move your fingers and wiggle your toes as you open your eyes. Know that you are love and you are loved. Remember that you are not alone on this journey. All of the answers that you seek can be found within if you take the time to listen.

Questions to Consider

1. My favorite form of meditation consists of _____.

2. When meditating and connecting with my inner self, I feel _____.

3. While meditating, in addition to connecting with my Higher Self, I have also connected with _____.

4. During meditation, I connected with my guides and discovered _____

5. When assessing and reviewing previous experiences, I recall that I have received guidance and

_____.

6. I recall instances when the guidance was subtle, but became more persistent when I ignored it. During that instance, I _____.

Suggestions to Consider

Journaling daily is recommended as it will assist you. Write down your thoughts, feelings, and emotions. Pay attention to bodily sensations as well. Read back through what you have written whenever you are guided to.

Take time each day to connect with YOU, your inner self, through meditation. Meditation takes many forms. It can be sitting quietly, listening to a guided meditation, going for a walk, or spending time outdoors in nature. For some individuals, reading is a form of meditation. Allow yourself to just BE. Allowing yourself to listen to the guidance you are receiving and to be present assists you in your transformation.

Pay attention to the guidance you are receiving from your Higher Self, your angels, and your guides. Sometimes, this guidance is subtle and comes in whispers and gentle nudges. When we refuse to acknowledge this guidance, it becomes louder, more persistent and may feel like the proverbial push or shove. It is important to recognize and acknowledge the guidance you are receiving and give thanks for it. You may not understand the how, when, why, or what of the guidance yet you should acknowledge it and express gratitude for receiving it.

Affirmation to Assist You

Affirm ~ *My heart overflows with gratitude and joy. I am conscious of being present in this moment. I recognize the guidance I will be receiving. I am allowing myself to simply breathe. I acknowledge and appreciate that I am not alone for my angels and guides are with me always.*

Message to Uplift

Message for today ~ **Surrender & Release**

Shelly's insightful interpretation ~ The angels are reminding you to surrender and release anyone and anything that no longer serves you. Surrender your cares and worries to the Universe. Trust that all is as it should be in each and every moment.

Note: If this week's messages do not resonate with you, please practice discernment and choose not to accept them for yourself. I encourage you to go within to interpret the meaning of the messages for you specifically.

~ Chapter 2 ~
Opening Your Heart to Love

Love is, above all, the gift of oneself.
~ **Jean Anouilh**

I believe that there are truly two ways to view anything— through the eyes of love or through the eyes of fear. Fear comprises doubt, worry, insecurities, feelings of lack and less than. Fear resides in the lower energies, which is our human-ness or ego. Love comes from the heart and is a higher vibration. I view these choices and have labeled them *TEAM LOVE* and *TEAM FEAR*. When posing this concept to my friends and colleagues, unanimous opinions vote to be included on *TEAM LOVE*. During discussions, we also recognized that we do have moments of fear and doubt as well as the other emotions, but we aren't a regular on that team.

With that said, which team are you on?

You gain strength, courage, and confidence
by every experience
in which you really stop to look fear in the face.
You must do the thing you think you cannot do.
~ Eleanor Roosevelt

Being an active participant of *TEAM LOVE* begins with loving you and opening your heart to love. In doing so, you will discover your greatest gift of all—the deep connection to your Higher Self and inner knowingness.

Expressing love to others is vitally important. In doing so, we are opening our hearts to give love and to receive love in return. Love is a nurturer of the soul. Love ignites the flame within us. For many individuals, loving other people and our animal companions is easy for them. They find it easy to speak the words, "I love you." Some individuals choose to express their affection by simply saying "Take care." No matter the terminology, the underlying intent and emotion is palpable.

Typically, these same individuals may find it extremely difficult to love themselves and especially to express it. We tend to only see our self-perceived imperfections rather than seeing ourselves as a beautiful, unique, and miraculous creation. This quote by James Poland speaks volumes to the significance of this action.

Like the sky opens after a rainy day
we must open to ourselves....
Learn to love yourself for who you are
and open so the world can see you shine.
~ James Poland

Loving yourself first and I don't mean in a selfish way allows the love you have inside of you to expand outwards. Loving yourself first is imperative in order to love others. How can we love another without truly loving our self? When you open your heart to loving YOU, you will attract this same love back to you because of the Law of Attraction. Choose to see the love within everyone. Express your gratitude for their presence in your life. You will experience a renewal within your relationships and within your heart as well.

Lend yourself to others, but give yourself to yourself.
~ Michel De Montaigne

Wearing a rose quartz bracelet or pendant or carrying a chunk of rose quartz in your pocket is a tangible reminder of this love. Rose quartz is the stone of unconditional love and infinite peace representing both physical and universal love.

I invite you to look at yourself in the mirror and say, "I love you!" It may feel awkward, but the awkwardness will soon melt. You may laugh at the silliness of this exercise. In reality, you will probably become emotional as you allow the feeling of love to envelope you. Know that you are worthy to be loved by YOU. You are loving the very essence of YOU. In loving YOU, you will love others more fully and freely.

Open your heart - open it wide;
someone is standing outside.
~ **Mary Engelbreit**

Just as the petals of a rose opens, I encourage you to allow your heart to open fully. In doing so, this heart energy is in full flow. Being pure energy, whatever you think, feel, say and do has an effect on everything. Allow yourself to receive the same love that you are sending out. Embrace and bask in this love because you are love and you are loved. Believe it for it is so!

"Opening your Heart" Meditation

Take a moment to just BE. Sit in a chair with your back straight and your palms up (open to receiving).

Close your eyes. Relax. Breathe in deeply and exhale.

Imagine yourself in the most beautiful tranquil place. This is your safe haven, your nirvana, your paradise. Your senses are heightened as you conceptualize this utopia.

You may have strolled into a hidden garden nestled behind an English cottage covered in ivy. Discovering a bench, you choose to sit down amongst the flowers and savor the sweet scents.

The delicate fragrance of the roses and other flowers fill your lungs. As you sit and bask in this splendid aroma, it is time to ground your energy.

Envision tree roots coming up through your feet and a vine wrapping around your legs. This vine is extending upwards into your root chakra, moving up into your sacral chakra, moving up and extending into your solar plexus chakra and resting in your heart chakra grounding you in Mother Earth. Now, envision white light from Source consciousness coming in through your crown chakra, down into your third eye chakra, down into your throat chakra, and meeting with Mother Earth energy at your heart chakra. You are grounded to Earth and to Light.

Be mindful of your breaths. Feel your chest expand with the inhalations. Feel your chest deflate with the exhalations. Feel the love you have within you. Allow the essence of you to unfold and surround you.

This beautiful Divine energy surrounds your being. Allow it to envelop you fully. Open your heart to love. Be thankful for this moment and every moment. Allow this gratitude and love to flow freely through you and around you as you simply breathe.

Affirm ~ *My heart overflows with gratitude and joy. I am conscious of being present in this moment. I recognize that I am love and I am loved. I am allowing myself to simply breathe.*

Place one hand over your heart and feel the pulse of life within you. It is through your heart that you are connected to all things. It is here that you will find your truth. Open your heart fully and freely to love and all that love beholds. Love is a nurturer of the soul. Love ignites the flame within us. Allow the love you have within you to surround you. Feel the love wash over you in waves of bliss as it cleanses your body of any pain you have previously felt.

Just as the petals of a rose opens, allow your heart to open fully. Allow yourself to receive the same love that you are sending out. Embrace and bask in this love because you are love and you are loved.

Express your gratitude for the love that is within you and surrounds you. Once again, be mindful of your breaths. Move your fingers and wiggle your toes as you open your eyes. Know that you are love and you are loved. Remember that you are not alone on this journey. All of the answers that you seek can be found within if you take the time to listen.

Questions to Consider

1. When expressing love for others, I find it easy / challenging.

2. When expressing love for others, I feel
_____.

3. When expressing love for myself, I find it easy / challenging.

4. When expressing love for myself, I feel
_____.

Suggestions to Consider

Journaling daily is recommended as it will assist you. Write down your thoughts, feelings, and emotions. Pay attention to bodily sensations as well. Read back through what you have written whenever you are guided to.

Take time each day to connect with YOU, your inner self, through meditation. Meditation takes many forms. It can be sitting quietly, listening to a guided meditation, going for a walk, or spending time outdoors in nature. For some individuals, reading is a form of meditation. Allow yourself to just BE. Allowing yourself to listen to the guidance you are receiving and to be present assists you in your transformation.

Practice expressing verbally love for YOU. Look in a mirror and tell yourself, "I love you." You can do this in the morning when you are brushing your teeth and combing your hair. It's important for you to mean it. Allow yourself to truly feel the love you have inside of yourself. This exercise will make you smile. It may even make you laugh especially with your first attempt. Laughter is healing. You may feel emotional as well. Allow yourself to feel what you are feeling. There is no shame in crying when doing this exercise, and tears are cleansing. Cross your arms and wrap them around you giving yourself a hug! Breathe in deeply and exhale. All is well.

Affirmation to Assist You

Affirm ~ *My heart overflows with gratitude and joy. I am conscious of being present in this moment. I recognize that I am love and I am loved. I am allowing myself to simply breathe.*

Message to Uplift

Message for today ~ **Guardian Angel**

Shelly's insightful interpretation ~ The angels are acknowledging your guardian angel. You are safe, secure, protected and loved. You are not alone.

Note: If this week's messages do not resonate with you, please practice discernment and choose not to accept them for yourself. I encourage you to go within to interpret the meaning of the messages for you specifically.

~ Chapter 3 ~
The Truth of Who You Are

We are all part of creation,
all kings, all poets, all musicians;
we have only to open up,
to discover, what is already there.
~ **Henry Miller**

I remember, even as far back as when I was a child, wondering exactly what my purpose is in this life. I asked the questions we all ask— Who am I? Why am I here? What am I supposed to be doing? Is this all there is? What's next?

Who am I?

I know that I am a woman, a wife, a mother, a

daughter, a sister, a friend, but who am I really? I am all of these and also none of these. The truth of who I really am is that I am a soul in a physical body having a human experience because my soul chose to be incarnated on Earth at this time.

I could go on to describe my physical body with height, weight, eye color, and hair color, but these are simply descriptions that will identify me. My likes and dislikes just happen to be my personal preferences. I am a soul having physical, emotional and mental experiences. The experiences I have had are just experiences. They do not define me nor will I allow them to. The memories of these experiences comprise the totality of my life as of this moment. As I continue to live my life, more of these experiences will encapsulate and become a part of my life yet will not define me. I am at the center of my consciousness, and I am aware that my perception— through my thoughts, emotions, and senses— creates who I am.

Why am I here?

I am here to acknowledge that we are all one— derived from Source energy. We are truly reflections of one another. I believe that I am here to shine my Light on others so that others can see the truth of who they really are while encouraging them to shine their own Lights bright. Through my words and actions, I am meant to heal hearts one by one by one and see people differently than they see themselves. I believe that there are two ways to view everything – through the eyes of love and through the eyes of fear. I choose to view life through the eyes of love and to assist others in doing the same.

What am I supposed to be doing?

As I reflect on my spiritual journey these past few years, my heart overflows with gratitude and joy. I am conscious of being present in this moment on this day, but I am also very excited as to what I see unfolding before my eyes. I see the direction my work is going. I am not controlling the aspects; rather I am allowing myself to be open to the idea of its ever evolving presence. In other words, I am not supposed to be doing anything. I am focused on simply be-ing and allowing myself to open to the flow and the realm of possibilities than anything and everything is possible. All we have to do is simply believe.

Allow yourself the opportunity to also embrace this clarity and greater knowing of who you really are. The knowledge you receive will help you to understand who you are, who you have been, and who you are becoming.

Seeing is not believing; believing is seeing!
You see things, not as they are, but as you are.
~ Eric Butterworth

Perception is how we view or perceive an experience through our senses— sight, taste, touch, smell, and hearing. We may choose to label an experience as good or bad, positive or negative. In reality, this is simply our perception or a personal assessment of the experience we have had.

Therefore, it is important to avoid labeling experiences as much as possible. If you can simply refer to an experience as an experience rather than labeling it as good or bad, you will change the energy of the experience. I am primarily referring to those experiences we choose not to repeat or the ones we label as "bad."

There is nothing either good or bad
but thinking makes it so.
~ William Shakespeare

Changing your perception assists you in changing your life. Remove the constraints of the box you have created for yourself, and allow yourself to view experiences with a new perspective as well as from another individual's point of view. Recognize that a group of people may have all had the exact same experience, but will each perceive the experience differently based on their own perspective.

Remember that each individual will have their own perception of an experience. It is next to impossible to alter someone's perception. In circumstances that you don't see "eye-to-eye," simply listen and then practice non-attachment to the outcome. This means that you are recognizing what you have heard, but you are not allowing another individual's perception to influence your own.

Furthermore, when someone asks for your advice or opinion, and they don't like what you have said, acknowledge the variance of opinions, and then release it. There is no need to feed it any energy or wonder if you should have said it differently. Speaking your truth with love and conviction is necessary. Do not be afraid to do so simply because you are not sure how the message will be received.

Once you awaken,
you will have no interest in judging those who sleep.
~ James Blanchard.

I believe that we plan each and every incarnation. We plan our challenges, our triumphs, and our opportunities for learning and growth. Most of us don't remember what we planned for ourselves. When we awaken to the truth of who we are, everything makes sense. We begin to understand why we chose our parents and our experiences. All judgment is released, and we are physically, mentally and emotionally at peace with our existence.

Earth school and all of the experiences it entails comprise our learning. Many of us definitely have a pre-conceived notion of how something should be or transpire. In reality, the Universe has something completely different in mind. When we release our expectations and the need to control the how, when, why, what, and where aspects of our lives, amazing things will and do happen. The unfolding is thrilling to see and to be a part of. Recognize that a path or plan may change along the way yet the purpose will not. All is as it should be in each moment of each life.

I recognize that I am Energy

Yes, it is true. We are more than a physical body. We must recognize that we are a spiritual being having a human experience. It is important to cultivate the Spirit, yet equally important to honor the mind and body. It is imperative to acknowledge that the mind, body, and spirit are one— a unified entity. Balancing the aspects of mind, body, and Spirit is an integral part of our overall well-being.

I recognize that I am Beautiful

As the saying goes, "beauty is as beauty does." A person can be perceived physically beautiful, but have an ugly personality meaning they are unkind and condescending to others. Our physical body is a protective shell for our soul. The beauty of our soul permeates this shell and that is what people truly see.

I recognize that I am Spiritual

To me, a spiritual person is someone who is walking their talk. They honor and respect other people's beliefs yet are true to themselves. They recognize that each one of us is a spiritual being having a human experience. Therefore, each person is having their own life experiences to learn and to grow.

I recognize that I am Authentic

I strive to live authentically in all aspects of my life. I recognize I was intended to have all the life experiences I have had and will have. I choose to view everything through the eyes of love rather than through the eyes of fear. I acknowledge that I am not the same person today that I was yesterday nor will I be the same person tomorrow that I am today. I am ever changing and every growing.

So I ask you, "Who are you really?"

"Discovering You" Meditation

Take a moment to just BE. Sit in a chair with your back straight and your palms up (open to receiving). Close your eyes. Relax.

Breathe in deeply and exhale. Imagine yourself in the most beautiful tranquil place. This is your safe haven, your nirvana, your paradise. Your senses are heightened as you conceptualize this utopia.

You may be walking on a beach at the ocean. You feel the warmth of the sun on your skin and the sand between your toes. The waves of the ocean gently and rhythmically make their way to shore. The salt air fills your nostrils as you savor the sights and sounds that surround you. As you continue to walk along the beach, it is time to ground your energy.

Envision tree roots coming up through your feet and a vine wrapping around your legs. This vine is extending upwards into your root chakra, moving up into your sacral chakra, moving up and extending into your solar plexus chakra and resting in your heart chakra grounding you in Mother Earth. Now, envision white light from Source consciousness coming in through your crown chakra, down into your third eye chakra, down into your throat chakra, and meeting with Mother Earth energy at your heart chakra. You are grounded to Earth and to Light.

Be mindful of your breaths. Feel your chest expand with the inhalations. Feel your chest deflate with the exhalations. Feel the love you have within you. Allow the essence of you to unfold and surround you.

This beautiful Divine energy surrounds your being. Allow it to envelop you fully. Open your heart to love. Be thankful for this moment and every moment. Allow this gratitude and love to flow freely through you and around you as you simply breathe.

Now is the time to discover who you really are in this moment. Choose to live a life of purpose. The core of your purpose focuses solely on your happiness and well-being. When you come from a place of love and see everything, including yourself, through the eyes of love, love is all that will exist.

What makes your heart sing and your eyes twinkle? Reach down deep inside of you and allow yourself to see that you are perfect in every way. See past the illusions and the self-perceived imperfections and discover the real you— the essence of who you are. You are beautiful! You really are! You are a miraculous creation. There is no one else exactly like you, which makes you unique. Discover who you really are.

Breathe in deeply feeling the embodiment of who you are. Divine love is truly the only reality. Everything else is simply an illusion that our human-ness creates. Focus your energy on being the best you can possibly be. Focus your energy on seeing and believing that you are a beautiful and miraculous creation.

Allow yourself to embrace this clarity and greater knowing of who you really are. The knowledge you receive will help you to understand who you are, who you have been, and who you are becoming.

Express your gratitude for this opportunity to discover who you really are. Once again, be mindful of your breaths. Move your fingers and wiggle your toes as you open your eyes. Know that you are love and you are loved. Remember that you are not alone on this journey. All of the answers that you seek can be found within if you take the time to listen.

Questions to Consider

1. Who are you?

2. When I think about who I really am, I feel _____.

3. When I think about what makes my heart sing and my eyes twinkle, I immediately think about _____.

4. When thinking about this, I feel _____.

5. Why are you here?

6. What are you supposed to be doing?

7. Have you been in a situation with others where you have noticed that you each perceived it differently?

8. When asked for advice or my opinion by others, I tend to _____ .

9. In doing so, I feel _____ .

10. What words do you typically use when describing an experience?

11. Do you find yourself using the words "bad" or "negative" rather than "good" or "positive" when telling others about your experiences?

Suggestions to Consider

Journaling daily is recommended as it will assist you. Write down your thoughts, feelings, and emotions. Pay attention to bodily sensations as well. Read back through what you have written whenever you are guided to.

Take time each day to connect with YOU, your inner self, through meditation. Meditation takes many forms. It can be sitting quietly, listening to a guided meditation, going for a walk, or spending time outdoors in nature. For some individuals, reading is a form of meditation. Allow yourself to just BE. Allowing yourself to listen to the guidance you are receiving and to be present assists you in your transformation.

Now is the time to discover who you really are in this

moment. Choose to live a life of purpose. The core of your purpose focuses solely on your happiness and well-being. When you come from a place of love and see everything, including yourself, through the eyes of love, love is all that will exist.

Message to Uplift

Message for today ~ **Spiritual Growth**

Shelly's insightful interpretation ~ The angels are acknowledging your spiritual growth. You are not the same person today that you were yesterday nor will you be the same person tomorrow that you are today. Keep going for you are growing!

Note: If this week's messages do not resonate with you, please practice discernment and choose not to accept them for yourself. I encourage you to go within to interpret the meaning of the messages for you specifically.

~ Chapter 4 ~
Being Mindfully Present

Light tomorrow with today.
~ **Elizabeth Barrett Browning**

The deeper I have delved into my spiritual work, the more I have realized the importance of being present. I have learned to appreciate each moment of each day as well as the necessity of balancing work with play and taking time for myself. For me, being present also involves forgoing technology whenever possible and taking a break from social media.

I have especially noticed the following scenario repeating itself. When I want to be on the Internet and Spirit doesn't want me to be on it, my internet connection slows down to the point that I get frustrated and get off of it voluntarily or it will have a "time-out" period and kicks me off. The feeling of frustration is more of a realization with a smile rather than animosity. I definitely recognize that this is their way of keeping me off social media and focused on the work I should be doing.

I recognize that whatever I post on Facebook, whether it is on my personal page or on one of my two fan pages, is being published on the front page of the "world newspaper" for all to see. I am extremely cognizant of my thoughts, words, and actions and the Law of Attraction. What I send out comes back to me.

As I am forging ahead, I recognize the need to allow myself to feel what I am feeling and to also establish better boundaries for myself. I have always been an extreme giver, and I acknowledge that I need to give to myself as well. I feel like it is necessary for me to do this because there is only so much of me to go around on a daily basis. I strive for balance rather than feeling pulled in all directions.

In addition, I found that it was also necessary for me to establish boundaries with friends, family and clients especially since I work from home. I have implemented work days and hours for myself and made them known. By respecting my own time, these individuals are respecting my time as well. I am vigilant about honoring others' boundaries as well even though they may not have verbally established any for themselves. I'm honoring their light as I desire my own light to be honored.

Furthermore, I really enjoy writing because it feels good to express myself. Many times, I feel like I "check out" and just write. The right words always come to me. I recognize that if I type the words that come into my mind, I can't go wrong. I have been using this strategic plan for years even before I was fully awake (spiritually conscious). I know now that it is a form of channeling or automatic writing. I am listening to the guidance I am receiving whether it is from my guides, angels or Higher Self. Utilizing writing as an outlet for me to express myself, I am tapping into the guidance I am receiving and conveying this guidance to others through written word. As I write, I am fully present in the moment.

If you worry about what might be,
and wonder what might have been,
you will ignore what is.
~ Author Unknown

As you re-read this quote aloud, listen to the words as you speak them and allow yourself to be fully present and ponder what you hear. Being mindfully present involves living in the moment rather than focusing on the future or dwelling in the past. Focus on living, being and breathing in the moment. As you become conscious of being present, your awareness will increase and you will become more connected with yourself and with others. Your appreciation for each moment will increase as well.

What lies behind us and what lies before us
are tiny matters compared to what lies within us.
~ Ralph Waldo Emerson

Being present also involves acknowledging, recognizing and then silencing the voice inside your head, otherwise known as mind chatter. Yes, mind chatter is exactly what it sounds like— the flow of words in the form of thoughts and questions that stream through one's mind continuously causing doubt and uncertainty. In yoga, this is referred to as "monkey brain." I named my mind chatter, Nancy, as in Negative Nancy. Her tone and voice sound like me, but slower and quite negative. The energy feels noticeably lower and sometimes even a tad bit mean. When I am feeling out of balance or stressed, she is present. When I am balanced and at peace, she is quiet.

Recognize that everyone has mind chatter. We have to acknowledge that mind chatter occurs and then choose to silence this chatter in order to derail its impervious plan. Perhaps, you may be guided to name your mind chatter just as I have. This mind chatter is comprised of a multitude of thoughts including memories and experiences that we have labeled unpleasant, which tend to remain in our subconscious and even conscious mind. These memories churn and simmer in our minds, resurfacing every now and again.

Individuals tend to replay scenarios over and over again and ask, "What could I have done differently?"

or "What if...?" They also play the "should" game saying, "I should have done this or I should have done that... then, this would not have happened." How can you be so sure? Hindsight, which is the ability of understanding later what was actually the best thing to do, is formidable. We tend to retain from experiences what is necessary for future growth.

In reality, the decisions we make at the time we made them are because we have freewill. Each one of us is having a human experience because we choose to. Learning from our experiences and not repeating them unless we choose to is a benefit to having them to begin with.

With that said, it is now time to forgive yourself just as you would forgive another individual. Do not admonish yourself for the previous decisions you made and now regret. Do not allow those experiences to define you. Release yourself from the pain, heartache, and frustration you have been holding on to. Silence the voice in your head.

I know what I have given you.
I do not know what you have received.
~ Antonio Porchia

In addition to the mind chatter, we have on-going associations with others. Present day communication surpasses just face-to-face contact. We can Skype, chat, talk on the phone, e-mail and text. The advances we have made in technology are nothing short of extraordinary. Effective communication involves communicating clearly, whether you are the sender or the receiver of the message.

I pride myself in being a good listener and communicator. I recognize the importance of clear communication. Clearly speaking or conveying the message via written means is only part of communicating clearly. The other part involves being clear about what you are expressing. Be sure and say what you really mean avoiding any doubt for the listener or reader. Be clear when expressing it. Sometimes, you have to spell-it-out and not be vague. Having to "read between the lines" inhibits effective communication— both for the sender and the receiver.

Miscommunication occurs because of our perception. In order to be an excellent communicator, it is essential as a listener to relay periodically what we have heard back to the individual speaking so that what is being said and being heard are the same. This is especially true when we get the feeling during the ensuing conversation that we aren't on the same "page." We don't always know how the message will be received so it's imperative to ensure that what we conveyed as the sender/speaker is what they received as the receiver/listener.

Once the message has been delivered appropriately, it is necessary to practice non-attachment to the outcome. This means that you are recognizing what you have heard and spoken, but you are not allowing another individual's perception to influence your own. This may happen when someone asks for your advice or opinion, and they don't like what you have said. Acknowledge the variance of opinions, and then release it. There is no need to feed it any energy or wonder if you should have said it differently. Speaking your truth with love and conviction is essential. Do not be afraid to do so simply because you are not sure how the message will be received.

In the hopes of reaching the moon,
men fail to see the flowers that blossom at their feet.
~ **Albert Schweitzer**

Awareness involves being conscious and utilizing your five senses— sight, taste, touch, smell, and hearing. Awareness includes being cognizant of your surroundings and the people coming into and leaving your life. The Universe will assist us in bringing people, teachers, and experiences into your awareness so that you can learn, heal, and grow. Be mindful of all that you are experiencing in each and every moment. Incorporating enhanced awareness into your daily life will ultimately enrich your life.

For myself, I have noticed that certain people will come into my awareness at exactly the right time for me to receive a message. The message may not be directed specifically towards me, but I receive it loud and clear nonetheless. I can almost feel a switch being turned on and off enabling me to glean exactly what I need. I recognize these as opportunities for learning and growth for myself.

Songs on the radio, television commercials, and even upcoming events are worth paying attention to especially if you keep seeing or hearing them repeatedly. Check in with yourself and assess if there is an underlying message or if you are intended to take it literally. Animal messengers and cloud formations as well as anything else that catches your attention should be noted. Symbols are everywhere and may mean one thing to an individual and something entirely different to another individual. Our perception assists us in our individual interpretation of these symbols.

Practicing discernment and what feels right to you is essential. In doing so, clarity of the mental, physical, and emotional bodies will occur. Silencing the mind chatter, communicating clearly, and becoming more aware will offer you this clarity. You will have a deeper understanding of your purpose here on Earth, and your Spirit will be renewed in every way.

"Awareness" Meditation

Take a moment to just BE. Sit in a chair with your back straight and your palms up (open to receiving). Close your eyes. Relax. Breathe in deeply and exhale.

Imagine yourself in the most beautiful tranquil place. This is your safe haven, your nirvana, your paradise. Your senses are heightened as you conceptualize this utopia.

You may be traipsing through a field of wildflowers. Their fragrant smell fills your lungs as you continue to breathe in nature. The blue sky is above you and meadow continues as far as you can see. As you continue to traipse, it is time to ground your energy.

Envision tree roots coming up through your feet and a vine wrapping around your legs. This vine is extending upwards into your root chakra, moving up into your sacral chakra, moving up and extending into your solar plexus chakra and resting in your heart chakra grounding you in Mother Earth. Now, envision white light from Source consciousness coming in through your crown chakra, down into your third eye chakra, down into your throat chakra, and meeting with Mother Earth energy at your heart chakra. You are grounded to Earth and to Light.

Be mindful of your breaths. Feel your chest expand with the inhalations. Feel your chest deflate with the exhalations. Feel the love you have within you. Allow the essence of you to unfold and surround you.

This beautiful Divine energy surrounds your being. Allow it to envelop you fully. Open your heart to love. Be thankful for this moment and every moment. Allow this gratitude and love to flow freely through you and around you as you simply breathe.

Now, open your eyes slowly. Focus your energy on being present and in the now at this very moment. Be observant and become aware of your surroundings yet allow yourself to simply be.

What do you see?

What do you feel?

What do you hear?

What do you taste?

What do you smell?

Allow yourself to become fully aware and completely present right here right now. Do not allow your mind to wander. Become cognizant of this moment. Breathe in deeply and exhale mindfully. Feel your chest expanding as you breathe in and your chest deflating as you exhale. Feel your heart beating rhythmically as blood is coursing through your veins.

Notice what you are seeing with your eyes and hearing with your ears. Be fully present and fully aware of your surroundings. All you should feel at this moment is being present. Continue being mindful of your breathing and relax. You are present in this moment.

Express your gratitude for this opportunity to enhance your awareness. As you continue to be mindful of your breaths, move your fingers and wiggle your toes. Know that you are love and you are loved. Remember that you are not alone on this journey. All of the answers that you seek can be found within if you take the time to listen.

Questions to Consider

1. When assessing and reviewing my current state of being, I tend to dwell in the past / live in the present / focus on the future.

2. When assessing and reviewing my current state of being, I feel _____.

3. How would you assess your communication skills?

4. Do you communicate clearly?

5. Do you listen effectively?

6. How would you assess your awareness level?

7. Are you adept at picking up on cues?

8. Do you tend to look for the underlying message also known as "reading between the lines?"

9. Do you tend to interpret messages at face-value only?

10. While spending time being cognizant of your surroundings, what did you hear?

11. While spending time being cognizant of your surroundings, what did you see?

12. While spending time being cognizant of your surroundings, what did you smell?

13. While spending time being cognizant of your surroundings, what did you feel?

Suggestions to Consider

Journaling daily is recommended as it will assist you. Write down your thoughts, feelings, and emotions. Pay attention to bodily sensations as well. Read back through what you have written whenever you are guided to.

Take time each day to connect with YOU, your inner self, through meditation. Meditation takes many forms. It can be sitting quietly, listening to a guided meditation, going for a walk, or spending time outdoors in nature. For some individuals, reading is a form of meditation. Allow yourself to just BE. Allowing yourself to listen to the guidance you are receiving and to be present assists you in your transformation.

As you are guided to throughout the day, find a quiet peaceful place that you can practice listening to the guidance you are receiving. It will be easier to hear when you are not distracted by outside noise. You may choose to meditate briefly or simply be present and listen.

Pay attention to the feedback you are receiving during communication whether it is in-person, over the phone or via written word. Being an effective listener may require you to relay back to the sender what you have heard and interpreted in order to make sure that you have heard the message correctly.

Increase your awareness level by focusing on tuning in with each of your five senses. Spend time each day being cognizant of your surroundings. What do you hear? What do you see? What do you taste? What do you smell? What do you feel? Make notes in your journal of your experiences as you are guided to do so.

Message to Uplift

Message for today ~ **Trust**

Shelly's insightful interpretation ~ The angels are reminding you to trust. Trust in the process. Trust that all is as it should be in each and every moment. Trust that all is truly well.

Note: If this week's messages do not resonate with you, please practice discernment and choose not to accept them for yourself. I encourage you to go within to interpret the meaning of the messages for you specifically.

~ Chapter 5 ~
Consciously Creating

The universe is change;
our life is what our thoughts make it.
~ **Marcus Aurelius**

Hearing the statement at some point along the way, "Your life is what you make of it" made me really question if I was truly living my life to the fullest degree possible. You mean it's not already planned out for me in its entirety? I can actually alter the course of my existence by the choices that I make?

When I was younger, I knew that I wanted to go to college, get married, and have two children as well as the proverbial house with the white-picket fence. Well, along the way, life happens and our vision becomes slightly altered, but we adjust accordingly.

The trick is in what one emphasizes.
We either make ourselves miserable,
or we make ourselves happy.
The amount of work is the same.
~ Carlos Castaneda

I somehow got caught up in the motions of a routine and began feeling less than fulfilled. Each day was the same - I would wake up in the morning, go to work, take care of my family duties, go to sleep, and then would start over the next day with the same routine. My vitality for life was nonexistent. Drudgery is a harsh term, but living life was feeling like a chore.

As a wife and mother, I tended to put everyone else before me. I was literally that pot on the back burner of the stove. The pot you stir occasionally, but aren't too worried about because you've kept the heat turned low. Well, sometimes we altogether forget about that pot, and its contents become scorched. It didn't take long for me to quickly realize that all the pots on the stove are equally important and should be stirred accordingly.

It's time to start living the life you've imagined.
~ Henry James

I took time to assess what I chose to change in my life; then went about creating this change. I quickly realized the importance of taking care of me, loving me for who I am and the impact that this has on my well-being.

In addition to returning to school to finish my college degree after a span of twenty years, I moved full-steam ahead with my spiritual studies. I became a Reiki Master and studied mediumship under the direction of world-renowned psychic medium Lisa Williams as well as with renowned medium and best-selling author James Van Praagh.

I am truly enjoying every moment of my life. I have met many amazing individuals and spiritual companions with whom I have shared meaningful and life-changing connections. Knowing who I am and where I desire to go in my soul's purpose, I look forward to waking up each morning and making a difference in the lives of others. My life is unfolding before my eyes, and I am so excited to be on this journey ~ this journey into consciousness! My heart is filled with joy and love as this journey continues. I am consciously creating my life and you can too.

What the mind of man can conceive and believe,
it can achieve.
~ Napoleon Hill

You are creating your reality. Therefore, you are a creator! The Universal Law of Attraction is a tool for manifesting. It is based on the idea that whatever we give a lot of attention to will become part of our lives. In doing so, we are co-creating with the Universe. What you focus on becomes your reality so it is very important to pay attention to your thoughts, your words, and your actions. Like attracts like. It is truly that simple.

As a single footstep will not make a path on the earth,
so a single thought will not make a pathway in the mind.
To make a deep physical path, we walk again and again.
To make a deep mental path,
we must think over and over the kind of thoughts
we wish to dominate our lives.
~ Henry David Thoreau

Be conscious of the thoughts you are having. Listen to the words that you speak and know that word modification may be necessary to avoid confusion and to be clear about your intentions. Becoming aware of the words you are using takes time and lots of practice. Listening to other individuals is much easier. I suggest that you really listen when others are speaking and pay attention to their word choices. It will assist you in becoming more aware of your own vocabulary.

In order to use the Law of Attraction effectively and efficiently, it is imperative that you clearly identify what you want, focus your thoughts on what you have identified, and then allow it to manifest. In other words, do not block the manifestation from occurring by infusing it with doubt, worry, and fear. Also, take into consideration that you will attract what you desire if it is for your Highest and best good. Release the need to control the details of the manifestation process such as the how, the when, the why, the what, and the where of it. Creation is happening very quickly as the Universe is working with you to bring your desires to fruition. Believe it, live it and you will manifest it if you are intended to.

Thoughts are mightier than strength of hand.
~ **Sophocles**

What I have come to realize is that life is truly all about making choices and then choosing to take action. When we align our thoughts, words, and actions with our beliefs and come from a place of love, amazing things will and do happen. We attract those people into our life who are a reflection of us. Assessing relationships and choosing to allow some relationships to run their course, so to speak, is necessary. As you make the conscious effort to maintain healthy relationships and end unhealthy ones, you are taking control of your life.

All that we are is the result of what we have thought.
~ **Buddha**

When we are in a state of bliss and peacefulness and offering gratitude daily, these feelings and emotions flow back to us effortlessly with ease. On the other hand, when we feel sad and lonely, these same feelings continue to swirl and twirl around us leaving us in this same state.

This wave of energy is assisting each one of us in rapidly manifesting what we desire. New people are coming into our lives just as people are leaving. Chaos is coming in for some people to assist them in clearing out the clutter. However, this chaos isn't something that we should be afraid of. Rather, I encourage you to recognize it, acknowledge it and then allow it to do its work so that you can move forward with grace and ease. It may feel painful, but I encourage you to see the light through the darkness and trust in the process. The process is making room for more light to enter. The changes may not be comfortable either, but they are necessary for continued growth.

Recognize that this is happening for a lot of people including myself. I feel like I am being presented with many opportunities for learning and growth especially by some of my friends and colleagues. I am seeing people for who they really are rather than the illusion they have created and are hiding behind. I am allowing myself to be mindful of my breathing rather than succumb to the emotions that are possible. I am surrendering to the Universe anything and anyone that no longer serves me or my Higher purpose. I am releasing it now fully and completely. I choose to create my life and all of its experiences consciously.

"Consciously Creating" Meditation

Take a moment to just BE. Sit in a chair with your back straight and your palms up (open to receiving). Close your eyes. Relax. Breathe in deeply and exhale.

Imagine yourself in the most beautiful tranquil place. This is your safe haven, your nirvana, your paradise. Your senses are heightened as you conceptualize this utopia.

You may have opted to imagine yourself in a winter wonderland. Walking in the gently fallen snow, you discover a frozen pond and reminisce of days gone by. Bundled warmly yet feeling the coolness on your face, you turn upwards as the snowflakes continue to fall and glisten in the sunlight. As you smile and relish in this moment, it is time to ground your energy.

Envision tree roots coming up through your feet and a vine wrapping around your legs. This vine is extending upwards into your root chakra, moving up into your sacral chakra, moving up and extending into your solar plexus chakra and resting in your heart chakra grounding you in Mother Earth. Now, envision white light from Source consciousness coming in through your crown chakra, down into your third eye chakra, down into your throat chakra, and meeting with Mother Earth energy at your heart chakra. You are grounded to Earth and to Light.

Be mindful of your breaths. Feel your chest expand with the inhalations. Feel your chest deflate with the exhalations. Feel the love you have within you. Allow the essence of you to unfold and surround you.

This beautiful Divine energy surrounds your being. Allow it to envelop you fully. Open your heart to love. Be thankful for this moment and every moment. Allow this gratitude and love to flow freely through you and around you as you simply breathe.

Affirm ~ *My heart overflows with gratitude and joy. I am conscious of being present in this moment. I recognize that I am a creator, and I am creating my reality. I am allowing myself to simply breathe. I am surrendering to the Universe anything and anyone that no longer serves me or my Higher purpose. I am releasing it now fully and completely. I choose to create my life and all of its experiences consciously.*

Now, allow all of your desires, dreams, aspirations and intentions to fill your conscious mind. Bask in the emotions you are feeling at this moment. Visualize yourself receiving and achieving all that you desire. Know that you are worthy to create the reality that you desire.

Express your gratitude for this opportunity to acknowledge your dreams and desires. Once again, be mindful of your breaths. Move your fingers and wiggle your toes as you open your eyes. Know that you are love and you are loved. Remember that you are not alone on this journey. All of the answers that you seek can be found within if you take the time to listen.

Questions to Consider

1. When utilizing the Law of Attraction, I recognize I am attracting _____ because that is what I am focusing on.

2. In reality, I wish to attract _____.

3. When assessing and reviewing my vocabulary, I recognize that I tend to use the following words repeatedly _____.

4. I typically say _____.

5. I will now say _____.

6. What do you desire?

How does your body react?

What is it telling you?

Do you become emotional as you read what you have written?

7. When assessing and reviewing my desires, I found it easy / difficult to list my desires.

8. When reviewing and assessing my desires, I feel _____.

9. What do you wish to achieve?

How does your body react?

What is it telling you?

Do you become emotional as you read what you have written?

10. What are your intentions?

How does your body react?

What is it telling you?

Do you become emotional as you read what you have written?

11. What do you wish to manifest?

How does your body react?

What is it telling you?

Do you become emotional as you read what you have written?

Suggestions to Consider

Journaling daily is recommended as it will assist you. Write down your thoughts, feelings, and emotions. Pay attention to bodily sensations as well. Read back through what you have written whenever you are guided to.

Take time each day to connect with YOU, your inner self, through meditation. Meditation takes many forms. It can be sitting quietly, listening to a guided meditation, going for a walk, or spending time outdoors in nature. For some individuals, reading is a form of meditation. Allow yourself to just BE. Allowing yourself to listen to the guidance you are receiving and to be present assists you in your transformation.

Take a moment to write down your desires, your dreams, your aspirations and intentions on a piece of paper. You are worthy to receive and to achieve all that you desire. A thought becomes tangible once it is written on paper. It takes form. You can see the words and touch the paper. Read what you have written and see how you feel when reading it.

Express your desires and intentions creatively. Creating a vision or dream board is a wonderful way to turn thoughts into words and pictures. You can flip through old magazines and cut out pictures or even search images on the Internet and print them off. Include any words, phrases, and quotes that resonate with you. Do not hesitate to think BIG either. The images you have chosen reflect your dreams— Dream Big! Your imagination is truly the limit; otherwise, you have no boundaries. Glue or tape the images to cardboard or poster board and hang them in a location that you will see throughout the day. Feel free to add or remove words and images whenever you are guided to as well. This is your creation!

Affirmation to Assist You

Affirm ~ *My heart overflows with gratitude and joy. I am conscious of being present in this moment. I recognize that I am a creator, and I am creating my reality. I am allowing myself to simply breathe. I am surrendering to the Universe anything and anyone that no longer serves me or my Higher purpose. I am releasing it now fully and completely. I choose to create my life and all of its experiences consciously.*

Message to Uplift

Message for today ~ **Nature**

Shelly's insightful interpretation ~ The angels are acknowledging nature. Spend time outdoors connecting with Mother Earth and grounding your energy. Be mindful of your breathing as you breathe in the fresh air. Doing so will refresh and revitalize your energy.

Note: If this week's messages do not resonate with you, please practice discernment and choose not to accept them for yourself. I encourage you to go within to interpret the meaning of the messages for you specifically.

~ Chapter 6 ~
Making Conscious Connections

We cannot live only for ourselves.
A thousand fibers connect us with our fellow men.
~ Herman Melville

My family and friends are a significant part of my life, and they are incredibly important to me. The resounding message, for most of my life, has been that people come into your life for a reason. It's not for us to determine what that reason is. Rather, we are meant to allow it happen— allow the relationship to unfold and see where it takes us.

Locating the tattered, type-written piece of paper (yes, I've had it for quite some time); I wish to share the content of a beautiful saying with you. The author is unknown.

People come into your life for a Reason, a Season, or a Lifetime.

When someone is in your life for a Reason, it is usually to meet a need you have expressed outwardly or inwardly. They have come to assist you through a difficulty, to provide you with guidance and support, to aid you physically, emotionally, or spiritually. They may seem like a God send, and they are. They are there for the reason you need them to be. Then, without any wrong doing on your part or at an inconvenient time, this person will say or do something to bring the relationship to an end. Sometimes they die. Sometimes they walk away. Sometimes they act up or out and force you to take a stand. What we must realize is that our need has been met, our desire fulfilled; their work is done. The prayer you sent up has been answered, and it is now time to move on.

When people come into your life for a Season, it is because your turn has come to share, grow or learn. They may bring you an experience of peace or make you laugh. They may teach you something you have never done. They usually give you an unbelievable amount of joy. Believe it! It is real, but only for a season.

Lifetime relationships teach you lifetime lessons; those things you must build upon in order to have a solid emotional foundation. Your job is to accept the lesson, love the person/people anyway; and put what you have learned to use in all other relationships and areas of your life.

As I am typing, I must reiterate and recognize that it is not important for us to determine whether the individual is in our life for a reason, a season or a lifetime. Only later, when the relationship has ended, do we discover why. Simply enjoy each and every moment of the relationship during the time that it lasts.

Throughout our lives, we have relationships with numerous individuals. These relationships may be labeled as passersby, acquaintances, friends, best friends, and intimate. Family members would also be considered, labeling as immediate and extended family. Of course, we will always be related to family members. Some family members may have differing beliefs than you and may even choose to vocalize these beliefs to you. How you choose to react to what they say and do is entirely up to you.

Although I was raised in the Baptist religion, I never felt like I had to go to church to connect with God because God was within me. I knew in my heart that he definitely wasn't the man in the sky. I believed that Hell wasn't below us and that Heaven was all around us. The destination Hell, for all general purposes, didn't even exist. For that matter, people could be living in hell on Earth. I acknowledged that Heaven is actually the spirit realm also known as the Afterlife.

I distinctly remember analyzing as a child how I could be alive— I am breathing, my heart is beating and blood is flowing through my veins. How is all of this even possible? I believe in reincarnation - my soul has incarnated for numerous lifetimes and will continue to do so once my physical body expires and I cease to breathe. I have chosen to be Shelly for this incarnation. The Spirit realm, also known as the Other Side, is literally right here all around us. Our loved ones no longer have a physical body and are vibrating as energy at a higher frequency than the earthly plane.

I realize that my beliefs will resonate with some individuals, but, more than likely, they will not resonate with everyone I know. I discovered that it is essential to honor and respect my own beliefs as well as others' beliefs. It is important to identify your beliefs, but it is equally important to acknowledge that not everyone has the same belief system as you.

When you live in reaction, you give your power away.
Then you get to experience what you gave your power to.
~ N. Smith

Understandably, the relationship with our soul or spiritual family is often times more fulfilling than the relationship we may have with certain family members. Acceptance rather than judgment is felt. We all deserve to be unconditionally accepted and loved. It is important to redefine the perception of family, allowing our personal perception rather than society's perception, to infuse our being. Many times, the relationship with our spiritual family may be bigger, fuller, and more expansive than our biological family. Living to have your life force constantly replenished rather than suffocated is a wonderful feeling.

*The energy it takes to hang onto the past
is holding you back from a new life.
What is it that you would let go of today?*
~ **Mary Manin Morrisey**

Recently, I have found it extremely important to clear the clutter, so to speak, in my relationships. I have found it necessary to assess those relationships that are healthy and balanced and those relationships that are unhealthy and draining. I made the conscious decision to cultivate the healthy relationships and place some distant in those relationships that I perceive to be unhealthy and imbalanced.

The Universe is truly assisting me in seeing people for who they really are without any illusions. I am becoming more aware of those individuals who are coming from a place of love and those who are not. I acknowledge that as I change, my relationships with others will change as well. I also recognize that the Universe is assisting me in clearing out the clutter in order for me to move forward with my work. For lack of a better word, the "dead weight" in my relationships is being cleared out as the Universe is literally making sure I recognize the individuals who are no longer in sync with me nor serve my Higher purpose.

Take control of your destiny. Believe in yourself.
Ignore those who try to discourage you.
Avoid negative sources, people, places, things, and habits.
Don't give up and don't give in.
~ Wanda Carter

I tell my clients, "Hold your heart in your hands and release everything that is not love— as love is all there is." This statement is a simple reminder to let go of anything and everyone that doesn't come from a place of love. The feelings of fear, anger, resentment, frustration, worry, and jealously serve no purpose in our lives. Relationships should be mutually beneficial on all accounts for all parties in every situation. Is this really possible? Of course, it is if the relationship is a healthy one.

Balanced relationships involve both giving and receiving. Just as in effective communication, speaking and listening is both required. Furthermore, when you give to others, you should also give to yourself. Invoking the Universal Law of Attraction, what you send out into the Universe comes back to you.

Wherever there is a human being,
there is an opportunity for a kindness.
~ Seneca

Bring this loving action into your daily lives. Realize that you are making a difference in the lives of others by being who you really are. Smiling, offering a kind word to another, and holding the door open are effortless acts that have meaningful results. Both the recipient and the giver walk away from the interaction feeling lighter and loved. No gesture is too small nor goes unnoticed.

Simply sharing a smile or offering a kind word will not only raise the recipient's vibration, but will also raise your vibration, as the giver or sender, as well. Practice compassion with everyone you come into contact including passersby in the store. Smile and say, "Hello!" It's really easy to do and both individuals will feel lighter and shine their own lights brighter!

Know that you are making a difference in the lives of others by simply being YOU. No extra work is required. By setting an example and shining your light bright, you allow others to do the same. Do not doubt the power that you hold within. In other words, quit doubting your ability. Choose to stop existing and start living. Live your life to the fullest. Enjoy each and every moment and don't sweat the small stuff. This is your life to live. When you start truly living your life, you will notice a difference. I assure you of that.

Acknowledging my own gratitude, I am so thankful for the individuals who have come into my life and the experiences I have had. I am elated to think about the conscious connections I will be making in the future as well.

On my Blog Talk Radio show, *Journey into Consciousness*, I share that, "My hope is to inspire passion, integrity and authenticity for all who share this journey. My greatest desire is to awaken the energy of compassion and connection, igniting the spark of Divine love and healing around the globe. The time is now and the power to choose is ours— ALL of ours. With an open heart and open arms, I extend my hand to you, inviting you to join me as we go forward together on this "Journey into Consciousness."

These words ring true if you allow them to. I invite you to join me in creating conscious connections with like-minded individuals who are walking the same path as you are. Recognizing your connection to those people who are in your life today will assist you in understanding the important roles we play in each other's lives. Please remember though to not compare your journey to anyone else's journey. Each journey is unique to that individual. We are all having our own human life experiences.

"Conscious Connections" Meditation

Take a moment to just BE. Sit in a chair with your back straight and your palms up (open to receiving). Close your eyes. Relax. Breathe in deeply and exhale.

Imagine yourself in the most beautiful tranquil place. This is your safe haven, your nirvana, your paradise. Your senses are heightened as you conceptualize this utopia.

You may be climbing a mountain in order to see its breathtaking view. As you tread softly being mindful of your steps, you ascend higher. Exhilaration is building you reach the peak. Standing in awe of the sight that beholds you, it is time to ground your energy.

Envision tree roots coming up through your feet and a vine wrapping around your legs. This vine is extending upwards into your root chakra, moving up into your sacral chakra, moving up and extending into your solar plexus chakra and resting in your heart chakra grounding you in Mother Earth. Now, envision white light from Source consciousness coming in through your crown chakra, down into your third eye chakra, down into your throat chakra, and meeting with Mother Earth energy at your heart chakra. You are grounded to Earth and to Light.

Be mindful of your breaths. Feel your chest expand with the inhalations. Feel your chest deflate with the exhalations. Feel the love you have within you. Allow the essence of you to unfold and surround you.

This beautiful Divine energy surrounds your being. Allow it to envelop you fully. Open your heart to love. Be thankful for this moment and every moment. Allow this gratitude and love to flow freely through you and around you as you simply breathe.

Affirm ~ *My heart overflows with gratitude and joy. I am conscious of being present in this moment. I recognize that people may be in my life for a reason, a season or a lifetime. I am allowing myself to simply breathe. I acknowledge and appreciate that when a relationship may end, it is making room for a new relationship to begin.*

Sometimes, we have lingering memories that remain in our subconscious and even conscious mind. They may be of individuals or experiences that we wish to release. Allow the memory of an experience or individual that you have labeled unpleasant to come into your consciousness. Do not relive the experience or try to remember the details. Simply allow this individual, event, or experience to come into your mind. Then, acknowledge and release this memory or individual you have labeled unpleasant. Say aloud, "I acknowledge. I release." Breathe in deeply and visualize yourself exhaling this experience or individual.

Continue to allow memories of an experience or individual that you have labeled unpleasant to come into your mind in order for you to release them. It is imperative that you do not try to remember the details of these memories. Simply acknowledge and release them. Breathe in deeply and visualize yourself exhaling this experience or individual.

Express your gratitude for honoring all of the

relationships in your life no matter the length of time. Once again, be mindful of your breaths. Move your fingers and wiggle your toes as you open your eyes. Know that you are love and you are loved. Remember that you are not alone on this journey. All of the answers that you seek can be found within if you take the time to listen.

Questions to Consider

1. When assessing my current relationships, I feel _____.

Are they healthy and beneficial or are they draining?

Are they balanced or a bit lop-sided?

Do you tend to be the one maintaining the relationship?

After spending time or chatting on the phone with this person, do you tend to be moody or do you feel joyful?

2. I acknowledge that I have healthy relationships with these individuals _____.

3. I acknowledge that I have unhealthy relationships with these individuals _____.

4. How would you assess your interaction with other individuals?

Suggestions to Consider

Journaling daily is recommended as it will assist you. Write down your thoughts, feelings, and emotions. Pay attention to bodily sensations as well. Read back through what you have written whenever you are guided to.

Take time each day to connect with YOU, your inner self, through meditation. Meditation takes many forms. It can be sitting quietly, listening to a guided meditation, going for a walk, or spending time outdoors in nature. For some individuals, reading is a form of meditation. Allow yourself to just BE. Allowing yourself to listen to the guidance you are receiving and to be present assists you in your transformation.

Assess the relationships you have in your life. In doing so, you may choose to allow some relationships to "run their course," so to speak. As you make the conscious effort to maintain healthy relationships and end unhealthy ones, you are taking control of your life. Remember, the Law of Attraction assists in bringing new people into your life as previous relationships come to a close. As far as family members go, you may choose to spend more time with some family members and less time with others.

Affirmation to Assist You

Affirm ~ My heart overflows with gratitude and joy. I am conscious of being present in this moment. I recognize that people may be in my life for a reason, a season or a lifetime. I am allowing myself to simply breathe. I acknowledge and appreciate that when a relationship may end, it is making room for a new relationship to begin.

Message to Uplift

Message for today ~ **Friendship**

Shelly's insightful interpretation ~ The angels are acknowledging the importance of friendship. Choose to cultivate the relationships you deem healthy and balanced. Choose to establish boundaries within those relationships you deem unhealthy and imbalanced.

Note: If this week's messages do not resonate with you, please practice discernment and choose not to accept them for yourself. I encourage you to go within to interpret the meaning of the messages for you specifically.

~ Chapter 7 ~
Awakening to Your Purpose

Twenty years from now you will be more disappointed
by the things that you didn't do
than by the ones you did do.
So throw off the bowlines. Sail away from the safe harbor.
Catch the trade winds in your sails.
Explore. Dream. Discover.
~ **Mark Twain**

As I previously mentioned, I often wondered as does so many other people exactly what my purpose is in this life. Why am I here? What am I supposed to be doing?

A very clear answer to these questions was revealed to me on May 1, 2008 through an angel reading with Steffany Barton of Angels Insight. After spending some time searching the Internet for someone to tell me about my angels and connect me with my loved ones who have passed, I found Steffany. I patiently waited two months for the appointment and recognize the date as a pivotal one in my life.

The reading began as follows:

> *I just have to tell you— you are a healer. Your soul is here to help change the world. You are a healer. You have come here to shine your light so that you can remind other people of the truth of who they are...you are here to shine your light so that others can remember the truth of who they are. You— allowing yourself to be a channel for spirit, allowing yourself to smile and to listen and to be available to people when they are in need and to see them differently than they see themselves. That's how you change the world and that's how you heal hearts, one by one by one by one...*

Hearing her speak those words, I literally had the cartoon-light bulb "Ah-ha" moment. As with so many other people, I know now that I was born during this period of time for a purpose. I became aware of this as I awakened to the truth of who I am. I began truly listening to the guidance I was receiving. Paying attention to this guidance, I delved deeply into my spiritual studies, in which Reiki played a defining role for me.

Signs have played an integral role in my ongoing spiritual evolution. On December 2, 2010, my day began with a short guided meditation and pulling a card for myself. This day I opted to use Doreen Virtue's Archangel Oracle Cards. The card I pulled for myself was "Spread Your Wings!" with Archangel Ariel stating, "Do not hold back right now. The timing is perfect, and you are ready to soar!" I accepted the message, but could feel the doubt settling in to my human-ness. Truthfully, I questioned my abilities and my purpose.

A few hours later, I walked down my driveway to get the mail. I clearly remember the bright cloudless blue sky. Walking back up the driveway and nearing the house, there was one cloud in the sky. I stared at it in amazement and smiled. The image from the oracle card was being presented to me "bigger than the sky." I ran into the house grabbed my camera and snapped a few photos. I went back inside to upload it on my computer. Returning outside to view the cloud once again, it was completely gone.

Now I should mention that there are naysayers when I tell this story. They say it was the trail left behind by an airplane. To me, the how or what doesn't matter. The Universe provided me with a sign. I promptly recognized this sign and expressed my gratitude for it. This cloud picture is my inspiration to continue to spread my wings and soar and to encourage others to do the same. I utilize it as my logo knowing that this message was the proverbial push I needed to get going.

Be yourself; everyone else is already taken.
~ **Oscar Wilde**

I personally believe that we plan each and every incarnation. We plan our challenges, our triumphs, and our opportunities for learning and growth. Most of us don't remember what we planned for ourselves. When we awaken to the truth of who we are, everything begins to make sense. In reality, all is as it should be in each moment of each life.

Earth school and all of the experiences it entails comprise our learning. I think we definitely have a pre-conceived notion of how something should be or transpire. I know that I used to. In reality, the Universe typically has something completely different in mind. With that said, allow yourself to open to the flow of what the Universe has in store for you. Recognize that your purpose may simply be to be happy and live life joyfully without regret. The interaction you have with others plays a pivotal role. When you offer a kind word, a smile, an ear to listen, you are making a difference in the lives of others.

Follow your bliss and don't be afraid,
and doors will open where you didn't know
they were going to be.
~ **Joseph Campbell**

As you awaken to your purpose, I encourage you to have patience with the process. Undoubtedly, you have heard the words, "Have patience," more times than you can count. I actually smile every time I hear the words just as I am smiling now because I have heard the words spoken so many times myself. It is essential to have patience with the process. Change takes time. Change doesn't happen overnight. Having patience is part of the process.

The path you take is made by walking it.
~ **Anonymous**

Do not get upset if you feel like you are not making progress. You absolutely are! Some days, you may feel like you are taking a step backwards or you may feel like you are having a self-perceived bad day. Honor yourself and what you are feeling. Take pause and rest when you need to. Don't think of the process as a game with an imposed time limit. As the saying goes, "Patience truly is a virtue!"

I am not afraid. I was born to do this.
~ Joan of Arc

Spiritual growth takes time. Remember, a seed doesn't become a flower overnight! It takes soil, water, nurturing, pulling the surrounding weeds, and sunlight. This translates spiritually to taking time for you as well as basking in the love and light! We can observe the change that is occurring, but the flower doesn't grow any faster.

It is also vitally important to remember that we are a continual work-in-progress, and there is always room for improvement. Each day is a new beginning. Therefore, with each day, each of us will have new life experiences. New experiences sometimes involve challenges. It's up to you if you view the challenge as the proverbial mountain or mole-hill. The fact of the matter is that it is all about perception. When you change your perception, you will change your life.

If we did all the things we are capable of doing, we would literally astound ourselves.
~ Thomas Edison

I recognize that I am not the same person I was yesterday nor will I be the same person tomorrow that I am today. My Spirit is continually healing and growing. I acknowledge the same for you. You are not the same person you were yesterday nor will you be the same person tomorrow that you are today. Your Spirit is continually healing and growing. Recognize your power and tap into your inner knowingness. Allow yourself to shine!

As your awareness heightens, pay special attention to the guidance you are receiving. The Universe is splendid when presenting us with guidance and signs. The ability to recognize when you are receiving guidance from the Universe, your Higher Self, your angels, and your guides is a skill that is easily mastered with practice and patience. Signs are presented to us as coins, songs on the radio, overheard conversations, and pictures.

Guidance is sometimes subtle and comes in whispers and gentle nudges. This same guidance may become louder, more persistent and may feel like the proverbial push or shove when we do not recognize or acknowledge it. When this happens, the Universe is adamant that we receive the message. It is up to each one of us to choose to listen and to take action on this guidance.

We have free will and can always choose whether or not to do so. However, it is important to recognize and acknowledge the guidance you are receiving and express your gratitude for it. Understanding the how, when, why or what is irrelevant at the moment it is recognized, yet it should be acknowledged. The significance will be realized at precisely the moment it should.

Pay special attention to the guidance you are receiving from your inner self. This is your gut instinct, which is located in your solar plexus chakra. As you become attuned to listening to your body and what it is telling you, it will become easier to recognize the messages that originate from this area.

Have you ever felt nauseous or had "butterflies" in your stomach? This may be feelings of nervousness, or it may be your body's way of telling you something. The term, discern, means to distinguish or perceive clearly. Therefore, practicing discernment is the ability to perceive the messages your Higher Self and body are telling you. Take mental note of this guidance. It is up to you if you choose to listen and to take action on this guidance. You have free will and can always choose. Practicing discernment in daily life is essential. Listen to your inner self and your body as they will not let you down.

"Awakening to Your Purpose" Meditation

Take a moment to just BE. Sit in a chair with your back straight and your palms up (open to receiving). Close your eyes. Relax. Breathe in deeply and exhale.

Imagine yourself in the most beautiful tranquil place. This is your safe haven, your nirvana, your paradise. Your senses are heightened as you conceptualize this utopia.

You may be hiking through the woods on a well-worn and familiar path. The foliage of the trees is lush and green, providing shade and coolness as you embark on your journey. The sounds of nature are comforting and uplifting. As you continue on your way, it is time to ground your energy.

Envision tree roots coming up through your feet and a vine wrapping around your legs. This vine is extending upwards into your root chakra, moving up into your sacral chakra, moving up and extending into your solar plexus chakra and resting in your heart chakra grounding you in Mother Earth. Now, envision white light from Source consciousness coming in through your crown chakra, down into your third eye chakra, down into your throat chakra, and meeting with Mother Earth energy at your heart chakra. You are grounded to Earth and to Light.

Be mindful of your breaths. Feel your chest expand with the inhalations. Feel your chest deflate with the exhalations. Feel the love you have within you. Allow the essence of you to unfold and surround you.

This beautiful Divine energy surrounds your being. Allow it to envelop you fully. Open your heart to love. Be thankful for this moment and every moment. Allow this gratitude and love to flow freely through you and around you as you simply breathe.

Affirm ~ *I recognize that I am not the same person I was yesterday nor will I be the same person tomorrow that I am today. My Spirit is continually healing and growing. I recognize my power as I tap into my inner knowingness. I trust in the process as it unfolds.*

Allow yourself to open to the flow of what the Universe has in store for you. Recognize that your purpose may simply be to be happy and live life joyfully without regret. The interaction you have with others plays a pivotal role. When you offer a kind word, a smile, an ear to listen, you are making a difference in the lives of others.

Now, pay attention to the guidance you are receiving at this time. This guidance may be from your Higher Self, your angels, and your guides. There is no need to determine the source. Simply receive and listen. Allow yourself to listen and to hear your purpose.

Express your gratitude for receiving the guidance you have received. Once again, be mindful of your breaths. Move your fingers and wiggle your toes as you open your eyes. Know that you are love and you are loved. Remember that you are not alone on this journey. All of the answers that you seek can be found within if you take the time to listen.

Questions to Consider

1. When assessing and reviewing previous experiences, I recall that I have received guidance and _____.

2. I recall instances when the guidance was subtle, but became more persistent when I ignored it. During that instance, I _____.

3. When you are in certain situations or around certain people, do you sometimes feel uneasy and want to leave?

4. Did you resist this feeling and decide to stay causing you to go against your inner guidance?

5. Do you recall feeling nauseous or having "butterflies" in your stomach?

6. When I assessed that experience, I remember _____.

7. I am familiar with discernment and I use it _____.

8. I recognize that I have received the following signs _____.

Suggestions to Consider

Journaling daily is recommended as it will assist you. Write down your thoughts, feelings, and emotions. Pay attention to bodily sensations as well. Read back through what you have written whenever you are guided to.

Take time each day to connect with YOU, your inner self, through meditation. Meditation takes many forms. It can be sitting quietly, listening to a guided meditation, going for a walk, or spending time outdoors in nature. For some individuals, reading is a form of meditation. Allow yourself to just BE. Allowing yourself to listen to the guidance you are receiving and to be present assists you in your transformation.

Take note of the guidance you are receiving. Silence your mind chatter and sit in quiet repose. As you become accustomed to paying attention, it will be easier to notice when you are not distracted.

Take note of the signs you are receiving. Remember these signs may be in the form of cloud formations, nature such as birds or butterflies, songs on the radio, overhead conversations, etc. Don't second-guess if you are actually receiving a sign. You may not understand the meaning of the sign at the moment you receive it. Simply acknowledge it, express your gratitude for it and you will understand the meaning of the sign when you are supposed to.

Affirmation to Assist You

Affirm ~ *I recognize that I am not the same person I was yesterday nor will I be the same person tomorrow that I am today. My Spirit is continually healing and growing. I recognize my power as I tap into my inner knowingness. I trust in the process as it unfolds.*

Message to Uplift

Message for today ~ **Study**

Shelly's insightful interpretation ~ The angels are reminding you to study. Listen to your inner knowingness and choose to study what resonates with you whether it be reading a book or taking a class.

Note: If this week's messages do not resonate with you, please practice discernment and choose not to accept them for yourself. I encourage you to go within to interpret the meaning of the messages for you specifically.

~ Chapter 8 ~
Shining Your Light Bright

This little light of mine, I'm gonna let it shine…
let it shine, let it shine, let it shine…

I remember singing these beautiful words in Sunday school when I was a child. As I am sitting here reflecting, I don't believe that I really knew at the time the poignant meaning behind these simple words. I remember that I definitely didn't feel like I was shining my light bright. I just happened to be singing the song.

As I mentioned before, I was conditioned as a child to mind my manners, keep my opinions to myself, and do as I was told. I lacked both confidence and self-esteem, and I was painfully shy. My light definitely was not shining very bright, and I am not sure that it was even shining at all.

Our deepest fear is not that we are inadequate.
Our deepest fear is that we are powerful beyond measure.
It is our light, not our darkness that most frightens us.
We ask ourselves,
Who am I to be brilliant, gorgeous, talented, fabulous?
Actually, who are you not to be? You are a child of God.
Your playing small does not serve the world.
There is nothing enlightened about shrinking
so that other people won't feel insecure around you.
We are all meant to shine, as children do.
We were born to make manifest the glory of God that is within us.
It's not just in some of us; it's in everyone.
And as we let our own light shine,
we unconsciously give other people permission to do the same.
As we are liberated from our own fear,
our presence automatically liberates others.
~ Marianne Williamson

Fast forward many years, I read Marianne Williamson's powerful quote, "A Deepest Fear," and discovered the significance of shining my light bright. Marianne's words had an enormous impact on my life the first time I read them. Actually, every time I read this quote, I have that same feeling of empowerment wash over me. It is the perfect reminder for me to shine my own light bright, and I encourage you to do the same.

There is a Light that shines beyond all things on Earth,
beyond us all, beyond the Heavens,
beyond the highest, the very highest heavens.
This is the Light that shines in our hearts.
~ Chandogya Upanishands

You may be asking, "What light are you referring to?" This light is your soul; the very essence of your being. Each one of us has the Divine spark within us. It is our right to be all that we are intended to be and so much more. As Marianne says, "We are all meant to shine, as children do. We were born to make manifest the glory of God that is within us. It's not just in some of us; it's in everyone. And as we let our own light shine, we unconsciously give other people permission to do the same."

Are you capable of doing this? Is it possible for you to shine your light bright? Don't hold back now. Put your shoulders back with your chest out and start shining your light bright! This is your life, you are creating it, and you have the power to choose how bright you want to shine. You are in control of your light. No one else is nor should they have the ability to control it. Do not allow anyone to dim your light under any circumstances for any reason whatsoever.

You who have the Light, what are you doing with it?
~ Paul Claudee

I have been tested on several occasions after choosing to shine my light bright. I did not evoke confrontation. Rather, I sent the individual love in each situation. I honored and respected their beliefs as well as my own. I realize that there will be many on-going tests, so to speak, and that it is extremely important to be true to myself all the while continuing to shine my light bright.

Our human-ness (ego) will creep in creating doubt from time to time—

Am I really worthy to shine my light so bright?

The answer is— of course you are! We all are!

The important thing is to recognize that this will happen and then acknowledge when it happens so we can move through these feelings rather than allowing them to manifest further.

> *To be yourself in a world*
> *that is constantly trying to make you something else*
> *is the greatest accomplishment.*
> **~ Ralph Waldo Emerson**

As I honor my own light, I also honor everyone else's light. As I continue my spiritual studies, I recognize that I may have growing pains. These "pains" or challenges are part of the growth spurt. I respect the emotions that I feel so that I can continue to grow physically, mentally, emotionally, and spiritually. I realize that I don't want to feel pulled in all different directions. I admit that I need to balance work with play. I know that I need to balance taking time for myself just as I take time for others. And, most of all, I understand that I need to honor the light within me so that it can continue to shine bright.

It's so important to believe in yourself.
Believe that you can do it, under any circumstances.
Because if you believe you can, then you really will.
~ Wally "Famous" Amos

With that said, I am paying attention to the guidance that I am receiving. I know and trust that all is happening exactly as it should in this moment and in every moment. What I have come to realize is that life is truly all about making choices and then choosing to take action on the choices that we make. When we align our thoughts, words, and actions with our beliefs and come from a place of love, amazing things will and do happen. We attract those people into our life who are a reflection of us. To connect with our inner light, we must connect with our heart and open our heart to love.

I am you ~ you are me ~ WE are one

"Honoring my Light" Meditation

Take a moment to just BE. Sit in a chair with your back straight and your palms up (open to receiving). Close your eyes. Relax. Breathe in deeply and exhale.

Imagine yourself in the most beautiful tranquil place. This is your safe haven, your nirvana, your paradise. Your senses are heightened as you conceptualize this utopia.

You may be standing at the base of a waterfall surrounded by lush green foliage. The sun is peaking through the canopy of trees. Listening to the sounds of the water rush over the rocks, you feel peace, pure peace. As this feeling of peace envelopes you, it is time to ground your energy.

Envision tree roots coming up through your feet and a vine wrapping around your legs. This vine is extending upwards into your root chakra, moving up into your sacral chakra, moving up and extending into your solar plexus chakra and resting in your heart chakra grounding you in Mother Earth. Now, envision white light from Source consciousness coming in through your crown chakra, down into your third eye chakra, down into your throat chakra, and meeting with Mother Earth energy at your heart chakra. You are grounded to Earth and to Light.

Be mindful of your breaths. Feel your chest expand with the inhalations. Feel your chest deflate with the exhalations. Feel the love you have within you. Allow the essence of you to unfold and surround you.

This beautiful Divine energy surrounds your being. Allow it to envelop you fully. Open your heart to love. Be thankful for this moment and every moment. Allow this gratitude and love to flow freely through you and around you as you simply breathe.

As you sit quietly, take a moment to perceive what your light is and what shining your light truly means to you. Appreciate the magnificent capacity you behold within you.

Let us now honor the Light within each one of us. Take a moment to recognize this light as you are grounded in both Mother Earth energy and Christ Consciousness energy. As you breathe in deeply and exhale, allow yourself to release anyone and anything that no longer serves you or your Higher purpose.

Affirm ~ *I honor the Light within me. I honor the Light within me. I honor the Light within me. Breathe in deeply. Exhale slowly and so it is!*

Express your gratitude for your light and its capacity to shine brightly. Honor yourself and your light wholly and completely. Once again, be mindful of your breaths. Move your fingers and wiggle your toes as you open your eyes. Know that you are love and you are loved. Remember that you are not alone on this journey. All of the answers that you seek can be found within if you take the time to listen.

Questions to Consider

1. I perceive my light to be _____.

2. Shining my light means I _____.

3. I recall these instances of when my light was dimmed by others _____.

4. I recall these instances of when I dimmed my light by choice _____.

5. Recalling instances when my light has been dimmed, I felt _____.

6. I recall these instances of when I shined my light bright _____.

7. Recalling instances when my light has been allowed to shine, I felt _____.

Suggestions to Consider

Journaling daily is recommended as it will assist you. Write down your thoughts, feelings, and emotions. Pay attention to bodily sensations as well. Read back through what you have written whenever you are guided to.

Take time each day to connect with YOU, your inner self, through meditation. Meditation takes many forms.

It can be sitting quietly, listening to a guided meditation, going for a walk, or spending time outdoors in nature. For some individuals, reading is a form of meditation. Allow yourself to just BE. Allowing yourself to listen to the guidance you are receiving and to be present assists you in your transformation.

Silence your mind chatter and sit in quiet contemplation. Take a moment to perceive what your light is and what shining your light truly means to you. Spend time in reflection and appreciate the magnificent capacity you behold within you. Allow memories to gently surface into your conscious mind of when your light had been dimmed by others as well as when you dimmed your light yourself by choice. Allow powerful memories to fill your body, mind, and soul of when you shined your light bright. Take note of any feelings you experience as you do so.

Affirmation to Assist You

Affirm ~ *I honor the Light within me. I honor the Light within me. I honor the Light within me.*

Message to Uplift

Message for today ~ **Celebration**

Shelly's insightful interpretation ~ The angels are acknowledging a celebration. Celebrate being YOU. See yourself as the Divine sees you – a beautiful, unique, miraculous creation. There is no one else like you nor will there ever be.

Note: If this week's messages do not resonate with you, please practice discernment and choose not to accept them for yourself. I encourage you to go within to interpret the meaning of the messages for you specifically.

~ Conclusion ~

Just as my journey continues, so does yours. My hope is that you have grown from what I have shared with you and that the insight and tools I have provided for you will continue to facilitate you on your spiritual journey. In addition, I encourage you to share your journey with others because we are all teachers just as we are students.

My motivation in life is to be happy and to live life fully without regret. As I have stated before, there are two ways to view everything— through the eyes of love and through the eyes of fear. I choose to view life through the eyes of love and to assist others in doing the same.

Choose to be present in this moment, right here right now. The past is in the past and cannot be changed. The future is yet to be created. All you have is this moment.

Allow yourself the opportunity to recognize that you are a spiritual being having a human life experience. These experiences may involve challenges as well as triumphs. Nonetheless, they are opportunities for learning and growth.

Choose to communicate your needs and desires to yourself and to others. This is your reality. You've got one "shot" during this lifetime as YOU. Enjoy it and have no regrets. In addition, make sure you tell everyone exactly how you feel. Leave no words unspoken.

Finally, know that you are having your own human life experience. Do not compare your journey to another's journey nor try to control someone else's journey. Honor yourself and what you are feeling at all times. Don't be afraid to ask for help and remember to love yourself always and in all ways.

Remember that you are not alone on this journey. All of the answers that you seek can be found within if you take the time to listen.

Much love and many blessings to YOU!

Shelly

I am the master of my fate;
I am the captain of my soul.
~ William Ernest Henley

~ About Shelly ~

Intuitive Medium, Reiki Master and Spiritual Teacher Shelly Wilson would love to assist you on your spiritual journey. With respect, truth, integrity and love, Shelly honors your free will and recognizes that you are co-creating your reality with the Universe.

She offers private readings, intuitive coaching, Reiki sessions, and teaches workshops.

The Shelly Wilson Show airs live each Wednesday at 2:00 pm CST on Blog Talk Radio.

www.ShellyRWilson.com

www.Facebook.com/IntuitiveMediumShelly

www.BlogTalkRadio.com/ShellyWilson

Books by Shelly Wilson:

28 Days to a New YOU
Connect to the YOU Within